POQUITO

UNPACKING
THE
MEMORY JAR

Copyright ©2017 by Tanya Montás Paris
Artwork created by Riris Nurul Awaliyah
ISBN: 9781730758492

POQUITO

UNPACKING
THE
MEMORY JAR

Tanya Montás Paris

For my siblings because the only place I
can see my true self is in their eyes.

For other writers who look and sound like
me because we too have our own stories to tell.
The spice of our tongues and the hue of
our narratives must continue
to forge spaces in the bookshelves.

INTRODUCTION

"You never told us that story" interjected teenager number two after listening to my explanation to a total stranger of the reasons why I became a vegetarian thirty years ago.

Goof, here are a few other little stories and bits of thoughts for you and for your big brother (and for any brave stranger out there).

CONTENTS

11

Chapter 1

**FRIENDSHIP
AND
KINDNESS
WITH A TWIST
OF HATE**

TURN BACK THE CLOCK

If I knew thirty years ago what
I know now. Oh, what a heck
of a friend I would have been!

FRIENDS

It's easy to make friends,
Keeping them? Now, that's a bitch.

MATH IS NOT ALWAYS AS EASY AS 1, 2, 3

The girl hates math. She sits frozen.
Her eyes blurred from staring at the two-page
document. The No. 2/HB yellow pencil is now
covered in small dents traveling up and down
in neat rows, a gift from her teeth, but she
pretends it's the imprint left behind by a legion
of rodents who had hungrily attacked an ear of
corn.

The pencil navigates to the palm, where she
slowly massages it, rolling it back and forth, a
movement sketched in her subconscious from
her primeval ancestors' practice of lighting a
fire.

She ventures to look up, only to find that
everyone else is putting their No. 2/HB pencils
to use. She brings the sharp led to the corner of
the paper and slowly traces over her name. She
turns to the next page, hoping for a miracle.
Maybe this time the writing would be gone,
leaving in its place just a beautiful drawing of
some sort.

The pencil feels heavy in her hand so she rests
it gently between the pages. She stares at the
eraser peeking out and feels sad. She feels she
has disappointed the eraser, prevented it from
doing its job. She picks up the pencil and erases
her name. She waits a little bit and then goes

back to the original corner and writes her name down; this time she does it in cursive.
"Five more minutes!" Announces the teacher, looking up from a book.

The girl stares at the writing and symbols decorating the pages. "Sorry," she whispers to the disappointed numbers as she furiously answers 2/HB on every question.

WHEN A SUPERWOMAN IS MARRIED TO ANOTHER SUPERWOMAN

I have a friend named Jen
She is a superwoman
I mean
Cracked skull from freak accident
She might never speak again
She might not be around to see the birth of her child
She might not be well enough to help care for her new baby

It just so happens that Jen is married to another superwoman

Upon facing love and super powers, freak accident had no choice but to revert its course

Now my friend Jen swirls about, dancing

in the sky with her super baby on her
shoulders

UNFRIENDING MY FRIEND

I have a friend who is kind of famous
He has a high-power job
He runs a high-powered company
He has a HUGE group of Facebook
followers

The other day he posted a video for his
wife's birthday:

"Un tributo de amor" he called it. Being
one to never pass on the opportunity to
watch a love tribute, I committed to the
ten long minutes and watched it from start
to finish.

It was incredibly beautiful, the way he
poured out his love for her, but then the
last five minutes he talked about how
beautiful she was and how he had asked
God for "Una Mujer Bonita" and God
came through by bringing this beautiful
woman to him. I went back and watched
the video from the start. I counted the times he
mentioned the word bonita and
the number of times he used the word
smart to describe his wife. The disproportion
was so unsettling and disappointing that I
clicked "unfriend"

"Maybe YOU just want your own tributo
de amor", whispers my sassy brain

A KIND WOMAN

One of the many lessons that I have learned
from my mother was to surround myself with
kind and smart women. I am lucky to have
learned that lesson early on.

In Elementary school, I found Eleida, Marilyz,
and Xiomara. In high school, it was the
friendship circle of Grisel, Marisol, Elsie, and
Lisania that carried me through those knotty
years.

In college, I held tightly like a barnacle on
Jenny, Helen, Cristina, and Laura who are still
my friendship pillars. There were, however,
many other kind and smart women who I
followed around one time or another, and even
though they are no longer in my life, I have
much to thank them for.

One of these women sat next to me in our
Education Research class during my senior
year in college. Over the years, I have tried to
conjure her name or at least details of her face,
but it has all escaped my memory. One day I
sat in one of the overstuffed chairs in the
student center, completely lost in pages of data

and clueless as to how to analyze them. Whether she saw it on my face or smelled my stress from where she sat, I will never know. She walked over and asked me about how the paper was coming along and I showed her all my data. She sat there for a while and then I showed her my paper draft. Then she told me that she was working on her paper that weekend and invited me to her house.

We worked all morning on my paper, then she fed me lunch as we continued writing, revising and highlighting passages from my notes. It was close to dinner time when we stopped and I collected my multitude of pages, said 'thank you', and walked out, too exhausted and relieved from having finished the paper, yet too self-absorbed to realize the gift I was just given.

I got an A on the paper

BEING PLAIN

"HE is so plain. It's like he just blends into the wall." I heard her say.

Was it that she felt that way about him that bothered me or that someone could think of me in that way?

I don't know who HE was, but I know who SHE is. I am certain that if she had looked closer, she would have seen some glimmer of spark of color. Yet, I consider, could it be her own plainness that prevents her from seeing the colors in others?

Then, of course, being able to blend into the wall might be a useful thing. Just imagine being at a party, standing behind a group of self-assured loud asses.

Ppprrrr! You go, releasing a rowdy putrid torpedo as you pull off your chameleon move, naughtily blending into the wall, plain and unseen.

ON THE INCA TRAIL

I walked behind a woman from Bulgaria on the Inca trail.

At some point, we came to a spot wide enough for more than one, and she slowed down and turned around. I greeted her as I passed and she made a comment about the weather and kept pace with me. She asked me about my hiking group and about what brought me to the trail.

I told her that my husband and our two teenagers were already way ahead of me. She told me that she was there with her husband

and that he was way behind her. Then she asked me about my teenagers and since they were not around to hear me, I told her all about them, I bragged and I vented.

Then she told me about her grown children, two sons, both married. The youngest lives in Amsterdam and is single. The oldest has a son. His wife is from Boston, but they have been living in Bulgaria for a couple of years now.

"What a treat it must be for you and your husband having your grandson around." I said to her, fantasizing about my own unborn grandchildren. Still swirling in my own fantasy,

I asked her if she would move to Boston once her son moved back. She stopped as if surprised by my question or perhaps she wanted to make sure I hadn't misunderstood her meaning. Between my Spanish accent and her Bulgarian accent, surely something would go astray. She said, "It's against nature for the cow to drink from her calf's milk." And that settled the conversation.

The trail narrowed and I stepped up my pace to catch up to my calves.

LOOKING GOOD
BY DOING GOOD

What if

Instead of our bodies being a result of what we ate and how we exercise, they were shaped as a result of our actions- the way we treated one another.

Buy a warm meal for a homeless person, next morning you sprout a beautiful new set of biceps

Feed a stranger's meter, that night you find yourself with a nice set of plumpy boobs

Donate toys and gently used clothes, Boom! There come those killer abs

Let people cut in line at the supermarket. Sweet! There are those defined thigh muscles you have been hoping for

No more "you are what you eat"; this time it's "You are how you treat"!

MIRROR, MIRROR ON
THE WALL

I wish to design a mirror capable of showing
the truth of how the world sees me

I would call on a person's name and my face
transformed into a monster would appear

I would call on another's name and a clown
would appear

     A vain thing? Sure!
     An evil plot? Definitely!

In knowing how they see me, I might truly see
them.

ON HATING

I have forever focused on LOVE
to the point of obsession

I have ignored its antonym completely
I am afraid of it
Avoid it like a rotting cavity
I happen to be an expert at cavities

I am a newbie at hatred

"Love TRUMP's hate"
"Hate does not live here"
"Hate cannot drive out hate"
"Free yourself from hate"
Confucius chimed in:
"It's easy to hate and it is difficult to love"
Yet, Martin Luther King, Jr. spoke
of hate being a great burden

Then it happened to me

I was ashamed of it
I blamed myself, "you are weak"
I shamed myself, "you are not the
  nice person I thought you were."
I scolded myself, "how could you feel
this way towards another person?"

Then I read a story about a woman
  who was also a beginner
She was also my age
She said, "roll with it".

I don't do well with hate, I am not sure
that I can yet roll with it, but I am
learning to let it visit, dance with it a
little, and hopefully it will go on its way.

THE MORE YOU DO IT,
THE BETTER YOU GET AT IT

"Want to be a good kisser?" Asked
my friend Cuchi,
then added "Practice with a mango"

I was thirteen
I am still practicing

LET ME OUT

It's small
Fragile
Trapped

It's confused
Lonely
Trapped

It's sad
Crying
Trapped

It's hurting
Disoriented
Trapped

It's not breathing
Shaking
Trapped

It's invisible
Guilty
Trapped

It's dying
Heart stops beating
Trapped

It's me
In a cage
Trapped

Chapter 2

AMOR Y MAS AMOR

JUST A LITTLE FANTASY

This morning I was awakened by an invitation

I accepted

I joined the delicious mating ritual
I exhaled when it was over

My eyes were still shut from the delirium when
he spoke

"Good morning, love" he said

The magic broke

It was my husband.

YO SOY

"What are you?" They ask, looking to
categorize me.

One answer could be, "I am an
anthropoid," but they will interpret that as
rude. So instead, I smile and say:

"Soy antillana por gusto y placer
Que goza la vida al amanecer
I am a traveler, the riachuelo's my guide
Soy la mazorca en el maizal
Concón tostado, carne guisada
Arroz con pollo y ensalada

"Soy lagartijas, cerezas, y mangos
Café con leche, huracanes y fangos

"Soy tamboras y palo
Maíz hervido y pan tostado"

"Soy huelgas a calles cerradas
Sol caliente, apagones, cubos de agua
Motoconcho y guagua"

"What am I?" you ask.

I am snow-covered hills and sticky
maple syrup
I am Whitney Houston, Jean-Luc Picard,
and the Fresh Prince of Bel Air
I am *The Wind Beneath my Wings*
and *Papa Don't Preach*

I am watermelon jolly rangers
and Birkenstocks

I am crackers, wine, and cheese
I am Challah, apples, and honey
I am McFlurry and French-fries

Next time they ask me, "WHAT
ARE YOU?"

I will stand tall and answer, "I am an anteater".

THE COLLECTOR

It is true
She likes to collect things.
She started her first collection when she was
eight; she collected party napkins.

Her collection matched her ever-changing
identity as she grew.

She collected masks when she was a teenager:
papier-mâché masks, porcelain masks, sequins,
and Mardi Gras masks.

On her first weekend away to Cape Cod with
friends, she fell in love with those small glass
bottles, so she began to collect them their
content as precious as the bottle itself: shiny
coins, shells, starfish, sand dollars, ships,

skeleton keys, paper scrolls, origami creations, and miniature figurines.

In college, she joined the International Student club and thus began her fascination with money from around the world. There were shiny coins in all shades of gold, bronze, and silver. There were small, medium, large, circular, octagonal, and square coins. She especially loved the coins with the carved out circles in the middle. Each place of origin showcasing a special symbol: palm trees, conquistador profile, lady liberty, koala bear, kangaroo, flowers, birds, even musical instruments.

There was a period when she also collected boyfriends: Dominican, German, African, Ecuadorian, Puerto Rican, African American, Irish, and Jewish.

Motherhood quickly swept into her identity. One day, she took her children to a beautiful river. She taught them how to "read" rocks: a wishing rock, a skipping rock, and, of course, the most precious of them all (in her opinion), a heart-shaped rock. She began her heart-shaped rock collection. Today her teenagers continue to contribute to that collection.

The collector became fascinated with bathroom signs; the pictures on the doors announcing the rule of who had access, with the underlying message of who was to keep out. Her favorites are the gender inclusive ones like the one she saw the other day, depicting a picture of a mermaid next to a centaur: *We don't care, just wash your hands*, read a sign above the pictures.

She became a traveler. She explored an erupting volcano in Costa Rica, learned to kite surf in the Dominican Republic, explored underground cenotes in Mexico, climbed Machu Picchu, explored the Amazon Rain Forest, and played on the beautiful beaches of the Caribbean islands. From all these places, she brought back a small bag of sand.

One morning she woke up and decided to free her hair. She stopped subjecting her hair to the toxic chemicals of relaxers and embraced this new identity with candor. But her curls went wild from years of servitude so she had to tie a long scarf around her head and off she went. With that grew a new collection, yes, scarves. And because her friends, her family, and her students notice "the scarves", the collection grew rapidly.

Now she collects happy wrinkles and friends. Oh yeah, and those beautiful 1920's mesh purses.

RAINBOW

Whenever I see a rainbow,
I wish I could stick a straw
in it and drink it all up

A WELL-MEANING DOCTOR

Once I went to the emergency room to get
stiches
The nice doctor tried to distract me while
sewing my flesh back together

"Where are you from?" he asked as soon as my
accent knocked on his tympanic membrane

"I am Dominican," I said, sitting a little
straighter, ready to represent Mi Gente

"Do you know that famous Dominican
writer?" he asked

I waited
No response
It's up to me to save him. To make him
sound like he knows something important
about my people

Could he be referring to old timers like:
Salomé Ureña
Juan Bosch

Pedro Mir
Fabio Fiallo?
Or more contemporary the likes of:
Junot Díaz
Angie Cruz?

Then I heard a butterfly whisper in my ear
and so I asked to the well-meaning doctor,

"Julia Álvarez?"
"Yes!" he responded, relieved
"No, I don't know her, but she teaches at a
college in Vermont where my husband went."
"A Dominican studying in Vermont?" he
asked.
"Yep," I said, giving up on the clueless doctor.

Note: although my husband's bachata
moves, Dominican-Spanish, and domino skills
have earned him the honorary title of "un
tíguere Dominicano," he was born a Bostonian
Jew.

THE GIFTS

A few months into dating
He gifted me a pair of rollerblades
I gifted him four pairs of socks

A year into our relationship
He gifted me a pair of skis
I gifted him a gift certificate to a fancy
hair salon on Newbery Street

Five years into our marriage
He gifted me diving gear
I gifted him an acupuncture session
Ten years into our marriage
He gifted me a hiking backpack
I gifted him a tree hammock

Twenty years into our marriage
He gifted me a set of hiking poles and a Machu
Picchu itinerary
I gifted him a memory foam mattress pad

It is possible that we have been gifting each
other the wrong things all along

PACHAMAMA

I fell in love with PachaMama. Well, I fell in love all over again with PachaMama, it's just that I didn't know her by this new name.

On our last day of hiking the Inca trail, I chew on the small bundle of folded coca leaves the whole stretch of the way.

"It's used as an offering to PachaMama," the locals had explained at the start of our trek. So, when I came upon her throne in the heart of Machu Picchu, I was overtaken by the specialness of the sight. I stared at her and felt her staring back. A gentle chill traveled the length of my body. I swallowed the moment, breathing and feeling.

Then pulled out the mushed up pack of tasteless leaves and placed it ceremoniously at her feet while a million prayers of gratitude and pleas flew out of my heart to meet her.

I stole a quick touch and brought my hand to my heart.
> My PachaMama
> My Mother Earth
> Mi Madre Tierra.

PARA TI

He is here tonight
Yes, ha!
Darkness
Tierno
Strong
Dulce
Hold
Tight
Darkness
Tierno
Dulce
Hold
Loose
Together
Smile
Gentle breathing
Goodnight

GETTING OLDER

"I hate getting older!" shouts my mouth to the mirror.

"Growing up is learning to leave behind all unnecessary baggage, along with a set of lovely childhood footprints." My heart chimes in consolation.

FREE YOUR TETAS

Today I am giving my boobs a break

"Don't worry," I tell them, trying to address
their concerns
"It won't be a rackety ride or anything like
that"

They recoil complacently nestling closer to my
chest

I pull my red shirt over, the one with the small
buttons and the neckline, the one with the
North Face logo and penny-size stain (not sure
where the stain came from- a Savers purchase)

"What about the humidity?" They warn me
shyly (their true nature)
I think of the wet spots that are sure to form,
but decide that it's worth it.

I am about to walk out the door when my
teenage daughter notices my rebellion

"Gross, MOM! Put a bra on!"

I ignore her directive, knowing it comes from
the place of, "my mother is so embarrassing,"
and walk out into the world with my
unconfined chest.

"Let's go ladies!" I tell my besties

A complicit mischievous giggle passes between
them
The air feels a bit lighter

THE WAY HE HELD HER

Like he held her on the way to school, fingers
entrelazados, each digit knowing what role to
play

They laughed and walked fast
They talked and slowed down, neither one
wanting to miss a sound

Each time they stopped, they looked at each
other
Just to check
They never let go
Not even once

Like he held her on the long bus ride, a helpless
creature cuddled tight under his arms, only her
hair showing
Talking softly, almost whispering
Enjoying each other's existence
And always holding

Hold me like that

WHEN YOUR JEANS THINK
THEY ARE FUNNY

One Saturday not long ago, a full-grown
woman showed the whole town her tush

She woke up excited, thinking about her long
list of fun errands

She showered up and put on her favorite pair of
faded True Religion Jeans, the ones her friend
Jen always compliments her on.

The tight fit with the oversized back pocket,
hugging her back curve in a perfect,
harmonious shape.

All morning and all afternoon, she paraded
around town making her way in and out of
errands.

In the late afternoon, she put down her bags
and walked outside to the patio, where her
husband welcomed her with a fresh cocktail.

She sat on the red veranda chair and sipped the
refreshing liquid.

Her brain registered a coldness coming from an
unusual spot.

She thought she had spilled her drink into the
seat.
"Did I sit on something wet?" She asked her
husband as she stood up to check the chair.

Her hand traveled the length across her
buttocks

Resting on her bare right cheek. It was peering
out happily.

A NEW BOYFRIEND

Because when you are newly dating and your
boyfriend invites you to the lake, you say,

Sure!

And you dip your feet in the freezing water
pretending to enjoy the refreshing feeling. You
don't tell him that you find even the
temperature of your Caribbean water cold

Because when you are newly dating and your
boyfriend invites you to a weekend away
during a hot summer wave, to his summer
house announcing, "there is a great outdoor
pool" thinking that will serve to entice you
So you say:

Sure!

And you sit on the edge of the pool soleándote
and teasing the water with your feet while he
playfully splashes you, taunting, hoping you
will jump in. You don't tell him that you are
afraid of the deep end

44

Because when you are newly dating and your boyfriend takes you away to a beautiful resort and offers to pay for scuba diving lessons you say:

Sure!

And you practice in the pool with the other newbies. You don't tell him that keeping your head under water for more than a few seconds frightens the living Jesus out of you. Even later that night in the emergency room when you are laying down with your hindquarters exposed as the doctor injects you with some concoction to ease the hammering pain in your ear canal (trouble equalizing!), you still get up early next morning and off you go to explore the underwater world with your boyfriend.

Because when you are newly dating, you also say yes to snorkeling, sailing, whitewater rafting, waterfall sliding, and surfing

And you don't tell your new boyfriend that you never learned how to swim even though you grew up with a beach in your backyard.

AND SO WE DANCED

aha hah
I'm hooked on a feeling
I'm high on believing
That you're in love with me

sings Blue Swede and as the catchy
Ouga chaka ouga chaka voices spread
throughout the dance floor

I am swayed around in euphoric twirls by my
fresh out of the press husband

"Let's have a double wedding," my sister had
suggested.

Why not?

Lips as sweet as candy
Its taste is on my mind
Girl, you got me thirsty
For another cup of wine

We sing and dance while a thousand faces
stare back at us.

ON BEING A SHEEP

Sometimes when I am trying to fall asleep, I play a little game

Instead of counting sheep, I pretend to be the sheep

I hop and I hop, trying to jump over the wall
Deep sleep awaits on the other side

I continue jumping and hopping until I become so exhausted that I fall asleep.

COOKIES BAKE IN 12 MINUTES, BROWNIES IN 25

Once there was a woman who baked cookies for her boyfriend

The timer rang and she took out the baking sheet

A dozen misshaped, burned chocolate chip cookies sat there defiantly

That night her boyfriend came to visit. He walked into the kitchen.

He looked at the cookies and he looked at the
cookie maker

He took a cookie and ate it

"Aah, crispy," he offered with a sweet smile
I learned two things that day

One: Brownies take 25 minutes to bake,
chocolate-chip cookies take 12 minutes

Two: A guy that eats your burned cookies is
worth keeping around (wink!)

LOVE

My friend has a boyfriend
She loves him
He loves her
But he also loves another
And he loves him back

ON DATING

I dated a handsome fellow

He got angry with me when he noticed I posted
a picture of Jimmy Smits on my bedroom wall.
Tears clouded my eyes as I took the picture
down.

I took that relationship down as well.

I dated another handsome fellow

He walked into my bedroom one day and found
me dancing, a silk scarf swaying in the air
following the rhythm of my Caribbean hips

The large poster of Antonio Banderas plastered
on the wall smiled seductively back at me.

The handsome fellow stared at me in wonder
and smiled

I married him

MY ACCENT

"Where is your accent from? I am trying to
place it," she asks, thinking she is being
friendly

Don't be a fool; it's never your "accent" they
are trying to place It's the mouth that speaks it,
the larynx itself

I stop to think. The feeling is always the same.
The way this question travels into my ear canal
and down my throat, as if I am swallowing the
stars, one by one.

"What part of my accent would you like to
place?" I would like to ask her

Is it the pinch of cinnamon and hibiscus that
wraps around my tongue?

Is it the African drumming of the merengue
beat that makes my tongue dance to its own
rhythm?

Or is it the voices of the Taínos that lay
dormant under my tongue, silently sobbing as
the savage Europeans raped the beautiful
Quisqueya?

ONE IS MUCH LIKE THE OTHER

I am not a good writer, but I like to write.
Much the same way that I am not a good
runner, yet I find great joy in it.

There are weekend mornings when I lay in bed,
mapping out my running route. I picture myself
eating half a banana mashed up with a few
tablespoons of quick instant oatmeal, then
putting on my sneakers and stepping out the
door.

Yet there are mornings when I lay in bed,
savoring a story that is shaping up in my head,
unable to get up until a satisfying conclusion is
reached. Sometimes the story is so emotionally
draining, that I have to reach out for a handful
of pillowcase to wipe away the tears.

There are times when the two merge. And it's
like a perfect orgasm. Yep, just like it.

It mostly happens around mile four, when the
story is coming to a peak and I don't want to
cheat myself by wrapping it up too quickly,
catching a new thought with every stride. So I
invoke the running goddess and she responds
by propelling me forward to complete that extra
mile, allowing me to achieve a perfect release.

TO FEAR OR NOT TO FEAR

Fear?
I keep it trapped in a box under my bed,
guarded by snakes. Lots and lots of snakes

I let fear out by invitation only

WRESTLING WITH MY KITCHEN DEMONS

I have been a vegetarian for over 20 years. It
doesn't take much skill to steam vegetables,
boil rice and pasta, and sauté some tofu. The
reason I have been able to hide behind my
kitchen demons is quite simple... my husband is
a magnificent cook. "Well, duh, he has a
mathematical logical mind," asserted my
kitchen demons as an attempt to justify their
existence.

Then, a few months ago, on an otherwise
ordinary day, when I least expected it to
happen, I decided that it was time to exorcise
my demons. First, I tried on my apron. My
colorful embroiled Salvadoran apron has been
hanging in the pantry, looking lonely for all
these years. I am convinced that I heard a
happy liberating sound coming from it as I tied
its long, wavy ribbons around my waist.

Then I continued my redemption journey by attempting to make those Dominican dishes I learned from my mom back in the D.R. -- arroz con guandules verdes, habichuelas guisadas con auyama, and pescado guisado. My attempts were valued but the dishes were flawed. My husband and the children would comment on how pretty the dishes looked -- that was my hint.

This trial and lots of errors period continued for a while. Then, just when I was about to submit to the abyss my kitchen demons were dragging me into, a most magnificent revelation came.

I was walking down the kitchen isle at Targé when I saw the light. Lo and behold, I discovered the Crock-Pot. And it was on sale! Oh, what a beauty. I brought my shiny, red, Slow-Cooking Pot home. I worshiped the box as I placed it on top of the counter -- its new pulpit. It looked so perfect next to the coffee maker, which until that moment had been my favorite kitchen appliance.

My husband looked at my new purchase and then back at me. He tried to say the right thing, "Great idea, blah-blah-blah." When I knew that what he really meant was, "oh boy, now what?!"

Well, my Slow Cooker and I are doing just fine! We have this great relationship. I put all the ingredients in it and turn it on. When I get home from work and open the lid, a fabulous and magical vegetarian meal appears! Will I ever turn into a cooking diva like Silvia de Pou (the Dominican version of Martha Stewart)? I doubt that. But, of one thing I am certain now, there are those who cook and then there are those who... slow-cook.

FACTS

I don't like to get up when the sky is still dreaming
I would share anything, except a blueberry muffin or a smoothie

I walked the oozing ground and climbed to the canopy of the Amazon Rain Forest, yet I am terrified of snakes

I am fascinated by British accents. I sometimes practice in front of the mirror. I am partial to the phrase: 'Are you mad? Of course she is my daughter!'

I make a delicious Pollo Guisao, the Dominican way, yet I am a vegetarian

I hear music and my heart starts to dance. Sometimes my shoulders, hips, and feet follow and then I just lose control.

I love yard sales.

Once I had a big yard sale and made $50. Then
I left the rest of the stuff on the sidewalk with a
"FOR FREE" sign,
got in the car and went yard-sailing.
I spent my $50.
What?
I love yard sales.

WHAT TYPE OF TREE ARE YOU?

"What type of tree best describes you?" They
ask during a professional development training
and a shower of questions rushes through my
head.

Am I the tree that speaks of despair and
sorrow?
Of inner strengths and resiliency?
Of freedom of spirit?
Of jealousy and betrayal?

When the words of hatred and micro-
aggression come at me like sharp daggers and I
collect my dignity and shuffle it delicately
under my wings to protect it. What type of tree
am I then?

When another black or brown kid is gunned
down on the streets just because of the melanin

in their skin and my insides turn dark and
angry. What type of tree am I then?

When not one, but two friends take their own
lives at the ripeness of their youth because
depression is considered a taboo, not an illness
and I sob into the night, grieving for them and
their family. What type of tree am I then?

I wish I could answer, "I am the Dominican
Flamboyant tree that stands tall, showing its
burning strength and beauty."

But I consider the question and I will have to
pass.

I can't possibly be a tree.
I am and must be a forest.

KNOCK-KNOCK

A good idea woke me up in the middle of the
night

It was gone in the morning when I looked for it.
Would it try again tonight?
Maybe dress itself up and put on a bit of red
lipstick and a set of sparkly cat's ears?
Or would it go away to where other good ideas
go?

Back to the bottom of the pile to be grabbed by someone else?

Do ideas die? Do they resurrect? Reincarnate? Do they become withdrawn after reflection and try again by attaching themselves to other ideas? Or do they return in rage and knock you silly on the head until that light bulb finally turns on?

REMEMBERING
TO WALK BACKWARD

Sometimes when I go on long walks, I stop myself and turn around to face the other direction
Then I take careful steps as I walk backward

Passersby might wonder about this unusual practice. They don't know that I am forcing myself to think about where I have been. I have found that it is also a great way to help you find your way back when exploring the Amazon Rain Forest.

DE DÓNDE SOY

"Where do you come from?" They want to
know.
This question, an explosive torpedo to the ears
of those of us with colorful English accents and
sun-kissed skin.

I come from a house that smells of ripe guava
La puerta de tabla que suena al abrir
El patio de tierra lavado con cal

I come from a room where my three sisters
slept
A light in the lamp half full of propane

I come from loud noises,
radio guarachita
I come from guineo,
arenque, aguacate
I come from Yolanda,
 risas y caricias
I come from Don Tilo,
firme, estricto, serio
I come from lluvias,
bailando en el zinc
I come from dignidad,
value, honesty

A GIRL AND A TRAIN

One day a girl waited at the underground train
station downtown.
She waited for the D train to arrive

"What if I just get on the next train that
comes?" she asked herself defiantly

A few minutes later, she boarded the next train
The C train took her far away from her final
destination

She felt brave.

THE WISH

A girl was granted a wish so she jumped into it
with the magical glee of childhood

She wished for a Collective Dream
Where males, females, transgenders, bigenders,
agenders, intergenders, genderfluids, gays,
lesbians, babies, teenagers, and one-eyed dogs
dream of lying on the grass, staring up at an
endless flock of butterflies.

And as they watched their wings flutter, they
begin to move their own hands unconsciously
and in no time their pinky fingers hooked left
and right, as if mimicking the butterflies'
dance.

RACISM

It is your problem to solve

Yes, you
The white man sitting over there with the
expensive looking suit

Yes, you
The white lady with the white baby
 sleeping on the stroller, look up from the
glearing light of your cell phone

Yes, you
The white police officer patrolling the
streets, eyes scanning for particular shades
of colors

Yes, you
White lady at the store following me
around thinking I was there to sneak
something into my bag

Yes, you
Look at me
I am talking to you
White grandfather with the MAKE
AMERICA GREAT AGAIN on your
t-shirt, your chest pumped high up

It is your problem to solve

I will keep hitting the ball back into your
side of the court
You throw me hate

I throw you hope
Maybe, just maybe, the ball will hit
you smack in your head

This is your problem to solve

Chapter 3

**MY CHILDREN
AND OTHER
PEOPLE'S
CHILDREN**

NO SOY LA BABYSITTER

Their skin reverts to their father's pale
 skin in the winter
They have blond hair, like their father

I was a rubia once, but they don't
know that
Actually, I am still a rubia, if just by name
La Rubia de Yolanda, yes, my
mother's blonde

They speak the language of their father
Although at home they speak the language
of rice and beans
With an extra helping of sweet
arepa- abuelita's cornbread recipe

The color of their eyes navigate among
a sea of blues and greens, like their father's
I also have green eyes, but the ladies at
the library don't notice,

When you have dark skin, you don't get
 to be seen

"Are you the babysitter?" One of
the ladies asked

She liked the way I played with
my children

"Yes," I should have said.
"I am also their father's lover."

LAVA PIE- WASH FEET

There is a little town next to my hometown called Lava Pie.

Some people say that it was named that way because there used to be a little stream that ran down from the mountainside and into the edge of town. When the mountain folks came down into town for a Sunday stroll in El Pueblo, they would step into the stream, scrub their muddy feet and put on their best footwear as they stepped into the city.

We always pass through this town on our way to La Playa Nahayo, one of our local beaches. And many times, as we cross that stretch from the town into the countryside, I hear the thumping in my ear, Lava Pie, Lava, Pie, Lava Pie.

I wonder about a town somewhere named, **Lava Boca.**

A place where people would require going to wash their mouths before saying something hurtful.

Perhaps Lava Boca would be just a few miles away from **Lava Mano**.

A place for people to scrub their hands clean before striking others.

And not too far from there, perhaps you will find the town of **Lava Corazón.**

To love, heal, and forgive.

AGAIN AND AGAIN AND AGAIN

Knowing the heartache of parenthood:
Would I do it again?
Yes!
Incompetent cervix and all

SMOKING CIGARRILLOS
AT THE AGE OF SEVEN

Well, not really cigarettes
But the dark red rolled-up bud of a hibiscus
flower

We inhaled deeply and took small bites to
account for the burning ends, just like real
cigarettes behaved when smoked by the
adults around us

I wonder if the grown-ups ever noticed that
we were noticing.

NEGRO Y BLANCO

The devil, NEGRO
The angels, BLANCO
The Bad Guy, NEGRO
The Good Guy, BLANCO

The Black Plague, NEGRO
A Black cat, NEGRO
Blackmail, NEGRO
Black rain, NEGRO
A Black swan, NEGRO
The Black witch, NEGRO
Black mood, NEGRO
Black hat, NEGRO
Black-hearted, NEGRO
Black sheep, NEGRO
Black market, NEGRO

The White knight, BLANCO
A White horse, BLANCO
A White dove, BLANCO
A White hat, BLANCO
The White House, BLANCO
A White wedding, BLANCO
White coat, BLANCO
A White picket fence, BLANCO

What if we collected these images in a
single frame and clicked on the sepia photo
  filter?

THE JUGGLER

There once was a woman who found herself
married, with two children, and a demanding
job

One day, she awoke unable to get out of bed,
feeling caught up in an undertow of
overwhelmedness

She realized that she couldn't carry on, trying
to give her best self to all

She felt herself dividing into separate
horcruxes

She considered the *horcruxes*, reasoning that
they did not work out so well for *The One Who
Must Not Be Named,* so she devised an
alternative plan

She put herself on a yearly schedule and thus
would rotate giving out her best self

And since that day, every year on the first week
of September she made her plan, rotating
between the various demanding parties in her
life

It worked much like the Chinese Zodiac
The year of the daughter
The year of the son
The year of the wife
The year of the husband
The year of the friends

The year of the family
The year of the job/career
The rhythm worked well for a long
time, then her children became teenagers...

LOOKING FOR SIGNS

"¿Por qué no tengo pelo como tú?" Asked her
six-year-old daughter as she playfully dangled
her small fingers through the jungle of curls
atop her mother's head.

"Porque tu pelo es un chin como el de tu papá y
un chin como el mío," answered her mother,
trying to explain the magic of mixed-race

That night the mother stares at herself in the
mirror.

She sees the face of her own mother staring
back. She smiles at the reflection. She
remembers her daughter's question and feels a
pang of guilt. Her daughter will not experience
this. Then the mischievous twinkle that dances
in her eyes appears and she smiles.

Her daughter will recognize that in her own
reflection.

THEY STILL NEED YOU

There is great satisfaction upon hearing
your grown teenagers scream

"MOM, THERE IS A BUG IN THE
SHOWER!"
Sometimes I pretend not to hear their cry,
 savoring their need a tad longer

"MOM! THERE IS A BUG IN THE
SHOWER!"
"Coming!" I said, tissue-bug-catcher in
hand

Confession: I have considered sprinkling a
bug here and there just to remind myself
that they still need me.

ALWAYS MY BABY

"Come here, you!" I tell teenager number
one while planting a playful kiss on his
belly

"Stop, Mom!" he says and then goes on,
"All you do is love me no matter what!" he
tells me, pushing me away, but not really.

Yep! That's one more thing he won't be
able to complain to his shrink about.

THE PAINFUL TEENS

How quick it switches from your daughter
wanting to be like you to not wanting anything
to do with you

DOMINO

"Mata, repite y cuadra," I repeat like
a credo while playing dominoes with
our teens.

Yes, the most important things in life,
I learned from my mom and
being Dominican, that
includes domino.

On each turn, my husband slams
down a tile the way he had seen it
done for over a dozen years
under the shade of the limoncillo tree.

"Juega malo!" I scold myself loudly
after laying down doble-cinco. That's
what my brother Felipe would say
if he were watching.

Teenager number two puts down her
five-two domino and waits for
teenager number one to go. My
husband and I stare at each other,

"Trancó el juego!" we shout in unison
I stare at my double-seis and shake
my head,
"Juega malo!"

I NEED A NEW CAR SIGN

When teenager number one was born, a friend
gave us a cute car sign sticker that read, "Bebé
a bordo", a warning to fellow drivers of the
precious cargo sitting in the back seat of our
station wagon.

We are now in need of a new car sticker

Warning: Teenagers on board

Any generous friends out there?

MUECAS

Muecas are what we Dominicans call those facial expressions that speak a language of their own. Of course, like in every language, you will need those who understand for it to work.

Take **cortar los ojos,** for instance. I tried to teach our teens this skill the other day. Although they got the "concept," their "pronunciation" (meaning their action) took some practice.

When you **cortas los ojos**, you must engage mind and body in that sassy move, and if you are not a sassy person to begin with, just be aware that it will take you twice as long to master this action.

"Así," I instructed them as I fix my eyes, narrowed them deep, and turned my gaze abruptly to the side, followed by a quick jag of the head. They watched me and then I watched them try and try again, teenager number two got the hang of it, no surprises there.

"When you **cortas los ojos**," I tell them, "you are replacing the physical action of slapping someone on the face. So be careful who you use it with, as you might end up with the skillful type of slap that leaves the imprint of the five digits across your face with ring decoration and all."

My husband moves his lips rapidly from side to side, a mueca used to express incredulity.

I laugh.

I had no idea that all these years besides learning Spanish he had also been learning the Dominican language of Las Muecas.

THE JOY OF BEING A KINDERGARTEN TEACHER

At the art center:
Me: B, get down from the table. Use a chair for sitting.
B: How does she know I was sitting on the table? She is not even looking.
A: She has eyes at the back of her head
B: Oh! Like in her neck

* * *

At the dramatic play area:
K: G, you are so lucky. You have two moms.
G: Yeah, I know.
K: I only have one mom.
G: You have one dad too.
K: Yeah, but he snores a lot

Chapter 4

WATER-A
DANGEROUS
THING

THE TIME (I THOUGHT)
I ALMOST DROWNED OUR
DAUGHTER

The Talmud lists a number of things that
parents are obligated to do for their children.
No, it's not food and shelter or even love, as
one would imagine.

Instead, we are required to teach them morals,
values, the Torah, and TO SWIM!

So, when our children pestered us about the
latest toy, alleging, "I'm the only kid in my
grade who doesn't have one"
(Do they forget that they have two teachers for
parents?)

We knew they were lying through those
braces'-tangled teeth.

And each time they tried to pull that one on us I
wanted to say, "We taught you to be nice, not
to steal, to read the Torah, and to swim. Now
go and get a job." But I didn't say it

The truth is that I have always been fascinated
by this "teach them to swim" thing, so we
followed the Talmud and taught our children
how to swim. The Talmud, however, didn't
mandate that parents learn to swim

So, when teenager number two was about six,
she wanted to go down a high-up, crazy,

winding water slide and convinced me to go up with her. Our happy screams from the descent were quickly muffled when we splashed into the pool and I landed right on my bum. I sat under water unable to find my footing, yet incapable of letting go of my daughter. A voice inside my head whispered calmly, "let her go," yet my own fear of protecting her would not allow me to release her. After what felt like an eternity, I was able to stand. The first sounds to reach my ears were my daughter's happy shouts asking me to go back up again.

I tried to conceal my panic as we walked out of the pool, grateful that she had stayed behind, splashing away with her big brother and cousins.

I sat next to my husband shaking, "I almost drowned my daughter," I sobbed into the chlorinated towel.

"Honey," said my husband, confused, "she was above water the whole time and you were under water for just a few seconds."

It is strange to people to hear that I am from the Caribbean, yet I don't know how to swim, unless that person is also from the Caribbean and would just get it.

A secret understanding between us only

THE TIME (I THOUGHT)
MY HUSBAND ALMOST DROWNED
OUR DAUGHTER

Unlike me, my husband is a great swimmer, (he is a great cook too- I know, I am a lucky girl!) and because he is so comfortable in the water, our children learned to love being in the water since they were little, allowing them to become competent swimmers at an early age.

This came at a great relief to me, but also brought great worry, knowing from personal experience how treacherous and unpredictable a body of water could be. And so, a big scary moment came to be.

It was during our trip to Costa Rica. We took a day trip to a remote spot with fluid cascading waterfalls and great jumping swimming holes (Tarzan of the Apes type of place). Our eight-year-old water nymph asked her dad to climb up a small waterfall and slide down the rocks with her. My alert antenna went up as I watched them make their way to the top of the waterfall. They held hands and slid down together, pure joy dancing on their faces.

I watched my husband's head emerge in no time. There were a few seconds of waiting in which my heartbeat quickened, traveling louder and faster than the current under my feet. My gaze froze on the spot where my husband stood, an incomplete puzzle. Then her little head emerged. The current had carried her a little further down. She laughed with delight as she swam with determination back towards her dad and the waterfall.

De tal palo, tal astilla!

THE TIME I ALMOST DROWNED

I don't know how to swim. When I confessed this shameful secret to my friend, Jen, she offered to teach me. "Ok." I said, knowing that I would never put a friend through that. What if I drowned? I can't put THAT on a friend.

How do I know I will drown? Because I almost did, once.

I trusted the water and the way it wrapped around my body. It tricked me into thinking that I was a mermaid and its happy, rhythmic waves lured me deeper into the belly of the ocean, farther and farther from the safety of the shore. The realization struck me when my feet did not touch the bottom, and just like that, the world went silent. I held tightly onto the floating log, no longer the sea horse it had been just a moment before, now my only way to salvation.

That was four decades ago. This year on my 50th birthday, I decided to welcome water back into my live. I am gifting myself swimming lessons. *Mejor tarde que nunca*!

Chapter 5

PETS AND OTHER
CRITTERS
IN BETWEEN

PING PONG

When our kids were little they
asked us for a dog,
so we bought them a hamster

One day I took Ping Pong the hamster
to school
I got to school, parked the car, and
grabbed my school bag.
I forgot that my companion was in his little
cage on the back seat of the station wagon
He was quiet and I was preoccupied

When I got home that afternoon,
I remembered Ping Pong the hamster
It was too late; the summer heat had
done its thing

I buried him behind our shed.
"He ran away," I told the kids
Don't judge me

FINDING A FROG

I dug a hole to plant a bulb
The bulging eyes of a perplexed frog
stared back
I quickly covered the hole back
I padded the last bit of soil down
    and walked away
      I found a new spot and buried the bulb

A SPIDER MOVES IN

I found a spider in my hair
I watched the clever arthropod, as it
stood there among the rumble, uncertain
of what to do.

"Are you here by chance or by choice?"
I wanted to ask
I could tell it was not an adventurous
 creature
Otherwise, it would have burrowed
playfully over and under the fuzz to find
a cozy screw curl closer to the scalp,

It would have rested its abdomen
comfortably and got busy spinning away,
 creating its own little empire
But instead, it waited on the surface, as if
begging to be rescued

I counted to twenty
UNO, DOS, TRES, CUATRO, CINCO,
SEIS...

"Last chance," I warned, eying the thin-
legged visitor
The spider ignored me.
I opened the window, shook her off

And set her free

A MYSTERIOUS DEATH

I had a fish
It committed suicide

"Suicide does not exist among animals,"
my friend told me
I found its lifeless limp body on the floor
 below the fish tank

"It must have been hungry or confused,"
my friend told me
"Or maybe both," she eyed me suspiciously
Don't judge me

ONCE I RODE A HORSE – IT DIDN'T GO SO WELL

My dad loved horses. We had a farm growing up, but he kept his special horse in our backyard. My brothers learned to ride horses from an early age, but they were not allowed to ride the "special one." We girls never learned to ride at all. I am not sure why that is. Perhaps because our religion prohibited it with the need for striding and all, since we couldn't wear pants. Although my mom did manage to become a skillful sidesaddle rider. Anyway, when my little sister was twelve, she decided she would get her own horse. She loved horses almost as much as my dad did. She saved up her own money and there came Poco.

He was a docile and old-ish majestic sort of beast.
Sometimes in the late afternoon, I would accompany my sister as she rode, fed, and brushed Poco's luscious skin and long mane.

Then one day I let her convince me to take Poco for a ride

People say that animals can smell fear; well, Poco must have had a terrific sense of smell attached to those large nostrils because as soon as I sat upon his saddle, he took off as fast as a racing horse, as if he had been plotting this moment all along.

He seemed determined to win or at least to teach me a lesson.

And, as I bumped up the hill, trying desperately not to fly off his back, I heard my sister warning,

"¡Agárrate!" as she chased behind with her fancy riding boots.

Now I just look at horses from afar. Once in a while, I get a glance from a horse and I swear I see a conspicuous smile, as if it were saying, "I know about you and Poco".

A FUR THUMB (OR LACK OF ONE)

People say that if you are exceptionally good
with plants, you have a green thumb. I wonder
what it's called if your pets flourish under your
care. Is there such thing as a fur thumb?

Whatever the term might be, I am sure I have
quite the opposite of it. So no, I don't want a
fur thumb or whatever that is called. It's not
that I don't like pets. I love animals, as a matter
of fact. From hissing cockroaches to long red
worms. So how can it be explained that the
strangest of things happen to animals under my
care?

I found one of our hamsters one day cuddled up
in his cage with a broken back.

Peter the fish was found on the floor beneath
the fish tank.

Twitch the hamster's beautiful brown fur
turned snow white overnight. "Old age," said
the vet before sending him to a forever dream.

Sarah and Buddy swimming happily in their
tank, then one morning it was just Sarah. No
signs left behind of what was of Buddy. Was he
abducted? Was Sarah just pretending to be
happy with him?

Well, there was also THAT one incident when
someone left a hamster in the car. By the

time she remembered it in the late afternoon, its body was soft and lifeless. She buried it behind the shed and told the kids that he had run away. We don't speak of this, though.

Chapter 6

ENTRE FAMILIA

UNO DE ESTOS DIAS TE VAS A ENCONTRAR UN POLICIA

"One of these days you will find yourself a police officer," we were warned as children when we brought home something that did not belong to us, "me lo encontré," we would try to reason, only to be instructed to put the item right back where we found it.

You see, the reason why this saying still freaks me out is because I am one of those cursed people with the gift of finding other people's lost things. My friend says that there are people who actually get paid for finding other people's lost stuff. I should look into that.

Granted, most of the things I find are just crap: a comb, headphones, a baby sock, hair elastics, and so on.

But there are other times when the find carries some heavy moral decision and the voice of my grown-ups will resonate loudly in my ears, "uno de estos días te vas a encontrar a un policia."

There was that time I found a small diamond in a public bathroom at a coffee shop. I sat on the toilet for a while contemplating my options. Hand it to the store manager, but what if the manager pocketed it? I could leave it right there where I found it, but what if someone else found it and pocketed it? "It is probably not even a real diamond," I considered. So I took it home. "YOU are pocketing it?" my brain asked. So I took it back to the bathroom a few days later and placed it back on its original spot.

There was that time I found a Tiffany's pendant with the letter 'H' engraved on it. I held it. Thought about the owner: Heather? Hailey? Helena? Harriett? Helen? Hannah? Hillary? Hortencia? I left it there. I hope it was found by its rightful owner. Or at least by someone with an H initial.

I once found three dollar bills. They laid there waiting one after the other, as if set up as a trap. Well, I fell for it. I picked each and every one of those suckers up and pocketed them.

Once when I was in college I found a wallet on the back seat of a taxi. When I opened it to see if there was a number that I could call, I noticed a small piece of paper with a number on it. I called the number and it was a realtor. I explained the situation and gave her the name of the girl on the driver's license. The realtor had just met with the girl that day and was helping her find an apartment. She called the girl, who came with her dad later that evening to collect the wallet. There was a ten-dollar bill inside the wallet. My heart was beating fast as I waited for her to arrive. What if there had been LOTS of money in the wallet originally and someone else had found it and taken it all, but the ten dollars? It turned out that I had nothing to worry about. There was only ten dollars in the wallet all along. How do I know? "I only have ten dollars," she said to me as she opened the wallet and handed me the portrait of Alexander Hamilton. I took it at her insistence, not because I felt I deserved it, but because it meant a week of riding the bus to school instead of the 45-minute walk.

SO, the other day I was running home and I saw a wallet in the middle of the road. I stopped and decided to wait for the lights to change with the intention of going to fetch it. Then I just stood there considering what I would do with it once I picked it up. Hold it in my hand as I ran the three miles home? Call whatever number I found inside? What if there was no number? No convenient realtor piece of paper. What if the owner knew this is where he had dropped it and is driving back to retrieve it?

A wise-looking older gentleman was crossing the street and walking in my direction. "Aha!" I thought. "I don't have to wrestle with the decision alone." I pointed to the wallet and asked the wise looking gentleman what we should do about it and he responded, "Not my fucking problem."

MOTOCONCHO

There is a mark on the inside of my calf,
The burned spot from a motorcycle's
Muffler

It is the mark of the working class
Dominicans who have come to rely on the
motoconchos as the affordable way of
transportation.

It is a mark I wear proudly.

MY ABUELO CHANO

Chano, Mi Pa'i, mi abuelo, my grandpa.
He was my mom's father. He died at the
age of 98 (or algo así). We are not sure of
his exact age, since there was no record
kept at the time of his birth.

He was like a rare book. He did not have the
type of smarts that comes with schooling, but
he had the smarts that came from oral tradition,
the smarts his ancestors had passed down to
him. Mi Pa'i had a wisdom that he inherited,
yet as much as he tried to pass it down to his
children, out of eight, only my mother stretched
out her hand to receive some of it.

As children, we listened to him, not because we were good listeners, but because we were fascinated by the things he said, even now as adults, my siblings and I find ourselves quoting our grandfather. You see, he spoke in refranes (some form of parables). When kids would run around being rambunctious, Mi Pa'i would shake his head and warn them, "mucho gusto, trae disgusto." And it wasn't long before someone would end up crying.

CHASING FRENZY

Chasing dreams
Chasing kids
Chasing students
Chasing dogs
Chasing storms
Chasing health
Chasing wealth
Chasing deals
Chasing youth
Chasing shade
Chasing sun
Chasing rain
Chasing fashion
Chasing love
Chasing promotions
Chasing intimacy
Chasing thrill
Chasing Nirvana
Chasing rainbows

Chasing your meal. A hen on the loose who wants to live to see one more day so that it too could chase after her chicks and her own meal.

REGRETS

I wish that I could tell you that I love you
I wish that I could show you appreciation
I wish the past wasn't so painful
I wish we could create a new beginning
I wish I knew you a little better
I wish you showed gladness of my being
I wish I could call you just to chat
I wish you knew about my sorrows

I wish I could look into your eyes and not
feel so small
I wish you wrote me thoughtful advice
I wish you knew what I've become
I wish you knew me a little better

I wish to hear that you love me
I wish you were so proud of me
I wish you believed in me.

DEL SUDOR DE TU FRENTE

For years we begged our mother for a TV,
"No hay dinero," she replied over and over, a
fact we knew only too well, nevertheless we
pestered her with our demand any chance we
got. Hearing the same tune from her seven
children finally wore her down.

But, my mother, is a clever woman, that one.
So she said, "I have a bag of squash seeds.
Let's plant them and with the money we get
from selling the squash, we could buy a T.V."
So it was settled. We worked long hours for
several months planting, tending the crops, and
finally selling the squash.

We got a small T.V.
We also got new school uniforms, school
 supplies, and a gas stove.
We also stopped pestering our mother to
buy us things.

MY TÍA TATICA

There is a Tatica in every family.
"Esa Tatica," my mother offers lovingly right
before she tells us the story (for the millionth
time) of her older sister. So she goes on
describing how Tía Tatica climbed up the
coconut tree, which she had been strictly
prohibited from doing. Their uncle came
looking for her, only to find her perched atop
the tree of life. When she refused his order that
she should climb down, he took his belt in his
hand, a sign of what was to come once she
descended. At this point, my mother pauses,
emphasizing that any reasonable child would
just obey and climb down, "Pero, no Tatica,"
she declares, explaining how Tía Tatica saw the

threat as a challenge and so she climbed higher, resting comfortably among the nest of coconuts. Now my mom explained that any reasonable adult would have left and gone on with their adult life, but instead, their uncle decided to defy his niece and settled himself at the foot of the tree, "aquí abajo te espero." My mom imitates her uncle's warning and then continues on with the story.

We listen to her tell the story and wait for the punch line, "so she peed down onto our uncle's head," she declares, shaking her head as if she could still see that very moment so many rainy days ago.

"Esa Tatica", she says again, and this time she wipes away her sad tears.

MY MC HAMMER PANTALONES

My dad was a spiritual man.
He was also very religious.

To that, throw in his law-abiding temperament and high moral demeanor and you cook up, well, my dad.

Like a true disciple, he firmly believed what was written in the bible L-I-T-E-R-A-L- L-Y. For example, there is a bible passage that considers women wearing men's clothes (pants, according to my father's religion) as an abomination to God.

And as a result, the women in our church, and by extension, my family were strictly prohibited from wearing pants.

When I came to the USA at the age of eighteen and settled in the January winter of Western Mass, pants became a necessity, but more importantly than that, the weather became the excuse I needed to FINALLY wear pants.

When I visited the D.R. after being away from home for several years, I wore my MC Hammer pants. I feared my dad's response and was prepared to take them off. I imagined him proclaiming, "las mujeres cristianas no usan pantalones." Yes, he truly believed that it was an unchristian thing for women to wear pants.

Yet, his response surprised me. My dad looked at me and ignored the harlequin attire as he embraced me the only way a father who missed a child would. I felt his love pour out and his happy tears spoke the rest.

I later heard him tell a neighbor, "I don't condone her pants."

Did he resolve to accept my pants revolt? Was he oddly confused by the crazy pantaloons?

My sister, Luli, would probably say, "he was happy to have you home," or perhaps my dad was also waiting for an excuse to transcend, to

be more open-minded. I chose to believe the
MC Hammer pants have given us both that gift.

MI MAMI

She's strong
Has always been
Her strengths, like splashing waves
She brings precious treasures from within
  and leaves calmness when she goes

She's pretty
Has always been
Her beauty se proyecta de muy adentro,
  carrying small residue of the Taino woman
It travels through her eyes como las olivas
vírgenes hanging proudly high on the olive
branches
They bring assurance and tenderness
Sorrows and worries

She is clever
Has always been
Nothing goes unnoticed, except when she
chooses

Esa es mi mami.

WATCH OVER MY DAUGHTER
(For my sister)

I am one of seven. It's the way I describe myself. A fact that frames my identity as much as the brown skin that wraps around my body or the tight curls growing stubbornly upward atop my head. And then, when asked: where are you in the line up? I answer like a credo, *Smack in the middle*, and THAT too is a key ingredient in the essence of who I am.

This is not something that I thought about much while growing up in the D.R. I mean, my siblings were just that, my siblings. A bunch of annoying multi-age kids that: were around ALL the time, got you in trouble with your parents, wore your clothes (even your brand new shoes!), read your secret crush letters, "borrowed" money from your acacia (our version of the piggy bank, made out of a recycled tin can), made fun of you in front of your friends, and the list goes on. But that all ended when we left our childhood behind and began to learn how to be adults.

It was then that I began to understand the bond. This is when the *I am one of seven*, started to take shape, to define me. It began with the birth of my niece, Yasira Margarita (Yasi), daughter of my oldest sister, Betzaida Margarita (que en paz descanse). Yasi was a premature baby who survived her twin brother. Her medical prognosis was concerning for the first few months of her life and through her infancy. She came to be known in our town as a miracle baby. Even if she survived, the doctors had warned my sister, there were sure to be physical or cognitive impairments. One of the doctors who assisted during her birth made monthly visits to our home to follow her progress. Yasi's health would become his charge for many years to come. As the next oldest daughter, the responsibility to help my sister care for young Yasi naturally fell on me as if there had been an unspoken agreement. I became her Mamita, her second mother. At times, when baby Yasi would throw a hysterical fit, refusing to eat her meals, my sister would turn to me with exasperation and concern. "Tómala!" she would plead with her outstretched arms. I would walk away and find refuge under the shade of a mango tree and try to cajole Yasi into eating her rice and beans.

As the young Yasi grew, so did the bond we shared. But another bond had also grown. It grew so quietly that I didn't begin to recognize it until years later. The way my sister would refer to Yasi when we spoke of her as if she were our shared responsibility. The way Yasi began to call my fiancé at the time, Papito, as if by default. The way my sister and I would talk about Yasi's future, even years after I decided to make the USA my new home and my fiancé at the time had asked Yasi not to call him Papito anymore since we were no longer together.

I watched Yasi go through her childhood years from the distant corner of Northfield, Mass. During those absent years when I couldn't afford to go home, my sister's letters and phone conversations were highlighted with stories of Yasi, knowing how much I missed her. The newspaper clippings of a chess tournament that Yasi won, or a Karate competition that Yasi participated in. And, of course, the reports of the perfect grades that Yasi earned in school, year after year. My sister would start our conversation with, "Esa muchachita tuya…" for, yes, it was true, Yasi was also *my little girl.*

Then I got pregnant with our son, Evan. It was a worrisome pregnancy due to my "incompetent cervix." However, after the anxious first few months and the tribulation of a cervical cerclage topped with months of bed rest, he was born a healthy baby (albeit with a little dose of jaundice). A few months after Evan was born, we traveled home to the D.R. for my family to meet him. My sister showered him with love and attention, but her health was already deteriorating and that would be the first and last time that Evan would feel her love. There were surgeries followed by hope, then more surgeries that shattered all hope. When it was clear that my sister was not going to survive the last round of treatment, I called Yasi, then a young teenager. Even now, almost twenty years later, I can easily picture where I was sitting when I made that call; in our living room holding the phone in one hand, while covering my face with the other, trying desperately not to break apart. Every detail of the room and of that moment is forever suspended in my subconscious, as it was the hardest conversation I have ever had to have with a person I love. And while my sister was resting comfortably on morphine at a hospital bed as her body settled into its final departure, my mom's hands lovingly intertwined in hers, I told Yasi what I knew my sister would have wanted me to tell her if her mind had given her the chance. *Your mom trained me to be your mom should there be a time when she couldn't be there for you. This time has come way too soon. Your mom would want me to take it from here.* The line went quiet; I heard her sniffles and then her dad's voice come on the phone. The truth was too hard for both Yasi and me. The grievous reality that she was losing her mother and I was losing my sister, shaking us both to the deepest of our cores.

It was around this time that I got pregnant for the second time. Just as in my first pregnancy, this one was also to be considered high-risk and like its big brother, this new baby was fighting an "incompetent cervix", the odds of a premature birth or a loss working against it. In spite of the worries, once again, I was able to carry full term and since I had also gone a week over my due date, a labor induction was scheduled.

Once at the hospital, my body began to feel the effect of having its water broken in addition to the intense contractions encouraged by the synthetic hormone, Pitocin. It did not take long for my lips to utter the magical word, "epidural." The relief brought by the numbing drug allowed me some spurts of rest while my body worked out its own magic of getting ready to deliver the baby. It was during one of these rest periods that I fell into a dreamlike state. In my chimerical dream, I heard hurried voices of concern around me. I saw doctors and nurses running in and out of the room while vital sound monitors beeped wildly. In the midst of the confusion, I saw a face, my sister's face. She was as beautifully kind and calm as she had been when she was alive. She smiled and said, "don't worry. She is going to be fine."

I walked out of the dream and into my reality to find my husband standing next to me. And before long, the "dream" became a nightmare. A nurse came, checked the monitor and left. Then she came again and quietly left again. The next time she came, she was followed by my OB-GYN. He informed us that the baby's heartbeat was irregular; it was under stress, and I would need an emergency C-Section. The anesthesiologist did his job and the nurse added medication to my IV. My husband's worried eyes locked on mine as the doctor described procedural details. This is the part where I should describe how frightened I felt, except that I wasn't. As the medical team brought down the curtain to block my view below my waist, I felt myself drifting into a sleep, a peaceful sleep as the dream of my sister rushed back to me. "Don't worry. She is going to be fine." I awoke from the procedure to stare into my baby's huge, bright blue eyes. I was not surprised when the doctor announced,

"Congratulations, you have a strong, healthy girl."

"Welcome Camila Margarita," I whispered as I held her to my chest.

I am one of seven. Seven: the number of days of creation. Seven: the colors of the rainbow. Seven: the number of circles forming the "Seed of Life." *I am one of seven* in spite of my sister's absence. The bond wrapped up in these five words continues to strengthen, like a cosmic truth. I will be turning fifty this summer, a reality that my reflection in the mirror reminds me of each day, even as my brain seems determined to hold on to the illusion of my much younger self. Yasi is now married, Evan is in college, and Camila is a junior in high school. This past Thanksgiving I was walking by Camila's bedroom and overheard my youngest sister, number six of seven, tell Camila the story of how, when she was single, she had worried about whether she would ever have children. She was describing a dream she had in which I had handed her a "seed" and how that had reassured her that, one day, one way or another, she would eventually fulfill her desire to have a child of her own, even if she had to 'borrow' my womb, incompetent cervix and all.

Where am I in the line up? I am *Smack in the middle,*

   I am one of seven.

MY TÍA TATICA AGAIN

Tomorrow is Día de Los Reyes, so today I will call home like I do every year as I run around the house preparing for our own celebration. In our American version of Three Kings' Day, my family comes over to our house the night before for a traditional Dominican meal of rice, beans, chicken, ensalada mixta, aguacate, tostones, arepitas de yuca, and pastelitos. This to be followed by arroz con leche and chinola juice for dessert.

We will gather in the living room and the kids will use the shadow box to retell the story of Los Reyes Magos (well, our family version of it). Then the kids will venture outside, trudging through the snow to get their offerings under the bed: grass for the camels (difficult under the snow-covered yard!) and candy for the Three Kings. Tomorrow we will get up early and enjoy a traditional Dominican breakfast of avena con chocolate and arepa while the kids open their presents.

But tonight we will also get a chance to retell the story of how we (my siblings and I) celebrated Día de Los Reyes as children. We each delight in the opportunity to relive those wondrous memories.

When we were kids, the day before Three Kings' Day brought as much excitement and magic as the day itself. We would walk miles in search of the right types of grass for the camels. It was a different spot each year. I remember one time walking to the edge of town by the riverbank. Someone had heard that tall camel grass was growing there, so off we went on our special quest. I don't remember what we found there, for as in any significant event, the journey was more significant that the actual result. There was a magical excitement as we each arranged our plate, our offerings. Grass and water for the camels, a green mint and a cigarette for the Three Kings (they must have been good at sharing!). That night we would go to bed early, "al que no se acuesta temprano, no le ponen reyes," warned the grown-ups, enticing us kids to get to bed early. In the morning, we would get up early to find our offerings gone and, in their place, a single toy. We would often get the same things: dolls for the girls and water guns or yo-yos for the boys. We paraded our Reyes (that's how we called our gifts) around all morning. Sometimes we would hear stories from kids who claimed to have seen the Three Kings or spotted a camel. And we believed them. After all, our Tía Tatica "almost" caught a Rey once.

"ESA TATICA," would begin my mother at some point during our conversation today. She would then describe how our Tía Tatica had hatched a big plan as a child to catch a Rey. She went to bed early and pretended to be asleep. She stayed up deep into the night.

"Mi Pa'i! Mi Ma'i! Despierten que agarré un Rey!" my mom would laugh in delight making her best impression of her big sister. And then, will complete the story with my favorite line, "muchacha sueltame!" my grandfather had shouted when Tía Tatica had attacked him, mistaking him for a King in the middle of the night.

OH, HAPPY SOUND

The rambling of the tires as they touch
the ground

The fierce wind fighting the arrival of
the large aluminum bird
It comes to a stop and the choir of
happy claps
Fill the belly of the plane

Welcome home, Dominicanos.

ÁNGELES AMONG US

I often hear, "we have too many labels," yet I
have been unable to find the right labels for
some very important people in our family. It
has always been hard to explain to people how
the Barretts fit into the fabric of our family. In
my own interpretation, they are the soft stuffing
inside the quilt that makes up our family, but
then I heard teenager number one deliver his
dvar torah, in which he so eloquently described
Joe and Marilyn as the angels of our family. So,
I am sticking to that label.

LA FINCA

We had a farm growing up. Much of our family
dynamic and, naturally, our siblinghood
identity have been intertwined on the
experience. From the many lawyers we had to
hire to help us deal with the number of
"friends" that my dad lent the finca to in an
attempt to help them provide for their family
and who then would go behind my dad's back
and try to sell the farm passing as the owner.
One such friend went as far as telling my dad
that the farm belonged to him because he had
been the one farming it. With each of these
conflicts, my brother, Samuel ('Reglamento',
my dad named him), would call a family

114

meeting and together we would hire a lawyer to sort out the issue.

My mom often jokes that the amount of money we have spent trying to keep the farm goes far beyond what it's worth, and she is right of course. But, here is the thing, it was through all these "deals" my dad got himself into that we learned the meaning of unconditional love, generosity, trust. We learned to work together and to rely on each other. That was my dad. It was the legacy he left us camouflaged as a farm.

MY SISTER, CARMEN

My sister, Carmen, is a beautiful soul. She often talks about Los Angelitos referring to the kind people that helped care for my dad. She is unaware that the biggest angel had been her.

LA LECHERA

One of my chores growing up was to sell cow's milk from our farm. My dad and my older brother would get up at the crack of dawn and ride down to the farm to milk the cows. My dad would stay back at the farm, tending the animals and the crops while my brother would ride the horse back with half a dozen gallons of milk dangling from the saddle.

Neighbors would come with their containers and I would measure out their portion, a cup of milk for 25¢. But most of the people paid on a monthly basis, so that money, or most of it, because there were plenty of people who couldn't pay once the month was up and my mom would pretend that they paid so as not to shame them and so I would continue to measure out their cup of milk each day just the same. Once in a while, a new customer would come in and pay cash. When that happened, I was allowed to keep 5¢. The leftover milk, I boiled for the family consumption.

There were periods when the cows were lactating so generously and we rejoiced in the abundance of milk. My sister would make cheese and butter and my dad would make his special dulce de leche. We kids would fight over who got to lick the pot!

So when I think about the time during which I was a milkmaid, the memory is matched to my father in our yard making his delicious dulce de leche. I can still both the memory and the sweet dessert.

ON CHOOSING THE RIGHT MATE

On the kitchen floor, I dance with gusto
accompanying Enrique Iglesias as he
passionately implores his lover to choose him:

Con él te duele el corazón
Y conmigo te duelen los pies...

Teenager number one comes in,
"Choose a partner that will make your feet
 hurt and not your heart ache," I tell him.

He rolls his eyes deep into his teenager
head and walks away.

Con él te duele el corazón
Y conmigo te duelen los pies...

Teenager number two comes into the
kitchen and I pause,
"Choose a partner that will make your feet
 hurt and not your heart ache," I tell her.

"Whatever, Mom," I think is what she
 mumbles as she walks away into her room,
leaving the loud bang of the door behind.

I play the song all over again and dance on
their behalf as I think about the many

aching feet I have gotten over the years
from their own father.

MOM IS ALWAYS RIGHT

Todos sentados
They are watching, waiting
"If they don't fit you we could exchange
 them"- dice ella

I won't take that chance
These are here
If she takes them, someone else will get
them, not me,

I will get nothing
"Muy grandes," she said, pointing at the
 inch-long gap behind my heel
"Just fine," I said, pushing back my foot
They are bright gold, too bright, I don't
care

I pretend to like them
"Why not another one?" asks one that is
 watching
"Oh no. These are just fine." Yo miento

I keep them
Not for long
Muy grandes
My mom was right.

CHASED BY A GHOST

She was ten
He was 60
She played with dolls and climbed trees
He had grandchildren of his own
She loved him
He took from her a sliver of her innocence
She lived her life in shame
A blanket of guilt casting a shadow over
  her soul

OUR OWN SET OF WINGS

My sister used to thank our dad for not
tying up our mother's wings.
For allowing her the space to capture the
wind and fly to her own altura, as high and
as low as she wished.

As my sisters and I began to grow our own
set of wings, we learned from our mother
how to spread them.

Flapping and fluttering them with care.
Flying tentatively at first and then surging
straight up with abandon.
Sometimes aimlessly, and sometimes with
eyes on a target.

Below us, our mother's wings flapping
vigorously, propelling the wind to keep
going.

Our dad's eyes and smile never leaving our
sight.

TRAVEL RITUAL

"Two suitcases and four backpacks?"
My husband asks himself on the passenger
seat as the teenagers and I settle tightly
into the back seat of a taxi on our way to
the airport.

Then he continues with his self-
interrogation:
"Boarding pass?
Check!
Wallet?
Check!
Phone?
Check!
Passports?"

He asks, then pauses to open his waist belt
to check the content for the tenth times this
morning.

He opens each passport ceremonially,
checks the expiration dates, and then

secures them back together with the elastic
band before placing them neatly back into
his travel pouch.

Check! He declares, having completed the
ritual.

BAD NEWS IN THE HAPPIEST
OF PLACES

I heard of my father's passing shortly after
arriving at the Sacramento airport after a five-
hour flight. We were on our way to a wedding.

We stayed the night at a hotel near the airport
and in the morning, I boarded the first flight out
back to Boston. I took a taxi home, grabbed a
bag that my niece had already packed for me,
and my passport, and got back in the taxi to get
to the airport to board a plane to the D.R. The
whole ride to and from the airport, my brother's
voice on the phone, calm and soothing, kept me
afloat.

We often complain about the annoyance of
airports: the waiting, the lines, the lost luggage,
the late flights, the canceled flights, the
overbooking, the change of boarding gates, and
so on.

And so, those are the things that I had thought of when thinking about airports, until that day when my father died.

You see, I never thought much about the travelers as individuals, each bringing in with them their own stories of happiness- a wedding, vacation, adoption, or others carrying a deep sorrow like mourning a loved one.

As I walked around, numb from sadness, engorged in a fog of despair, I began to see people differently. It was as if death had gifted me the right to see it dragging behind others. Much like the *thestrals* being visible to Luna Lovegood and Harry Potter.

Today as I was walking to our gate, I noticed a woman crying. There was no sound. The dabbing of her eyes gave it away.

I watched her from afar, unable to move my gaze.

Hoping that she would notice me so that I could telepathically tell her that I was sorry for her sorrow.

Perhaps I should have just walked over and offered her a clean tissue or a bottled water.

I would have welcomed a friendly hand squeeze myself. Next time I will do just that.

MY MOTHER'S DAUGHTER

The other day I looked in the mirror
and my mother's face stared back

We both smiled

SOMETIMES A MINUTE IS
MORE LIKE SEVEN HOURS

Today I sat down to write a quick thought
My husband called me down to dinner
seven hours later

THINKING OF MI PAPI

I was thinking about the tribulation
of life as I ran by a cornfield this
morning. That's when I heard my
dad's whispers.

La tierra, PachaMama, Mother Earth.
My connection to him. It was our common
language. Over the years, as I prepared our
vegetable beds, I would get on the phone
with my dad. I would describe the spots
and go over my list of possible crops:

Tomatoes
Basil
Lettuce
Corn
Okra
Potatoes
Pepper
Cilantro.
And then we would engage in a strategic
conversation:
"Acuérdate que el maíz son tres granitos
por hoyo y van en hileras." He would
remind me of the three kernels per hole
and the arrangement of rows to allow for
self-pollination. I know this well, having
helped with corn plantation as a young
 child. My dad up ahead in the field
digging the holes with an ax, we the kids
following each with a handful of kernels
piled up like a pouch inside our stretched-out
shirts. We would drop a trio of kernels, no need
to count them because our fingers had
memorized the quantity. Not far behind came
our mother, covering and patting down the
hole, setting the kernels comfortably.

We would continue on that planting dance all
day, only breaking for a lunch of locrio con
aguacate.

And, on the phone with my dad he would go on
with another suggestion and I would listen, and
take notes.

"Un buen abono de estiércol," he would advise. I put a star next to that. I will need to call our local farm and put in a special order for organic cow manure. Then we move to the molondrones and I remind him that the okra didn't do so well last year.

"Fíjate bien en las semillitas." He said as I open the small seed packet, not sure of what he was referring to.

"Por qué?" I asked, still puzzled

"Tienes que ponerlas en agua. Las flotantes bótalas. Solo sirven las que se hunden." He explained the trick of putting them in water and discarding the floating seeds, only the remaining heavier ones will be good for planting.

"Aha!" I smiled, savoring this new learning.

So, today as I run by the cornfield anxious about life's challenges, mi papi whispered a reminder and so I will continue planting only the good seeds.

CAT'S EYES

Her siblings named her Ojos de Gato
But it should have been her temperament that
was compared to the feline creature, not the
green shade of her eyes

The way her skin stands on edge, with touches
of off-putting. A sense of inquisitiveness, and
mostly friendly, but unpredictable and ready to
pounce.

Playful, loving, and independent, yet
demanding and expectant. With an air of
'LOOK AT ME, but on my terms'.

She is generous, but would mark her territory.
She prefers flower scents to urine, but still.

MOMENTOS DE ENSEÑANZA

She stole a tambourine once.
She was eight years old.
Her mom said,
"I will give five cents to whoever finds it."
All the kids started to look around the
house
A scavenger hunt of sorts
The girl followed the frenzy
She was good at pretending (or so she
thought)
Under the bed she went
"It's not here!" She declared aloud

126

Behind the refrigerator she looked,
"It's not here!" she announced theatrically
Then she rushed over to the bedroom she
  shared with her three sisters, her thin arm
  reached deep behind the bookshelf
"I found it!" she announced, proudly
banging on the tambourine on her way to
the yard
The kids yell excitedly
Her dad took out his belt
His face plastered with shame and rage
"No le pegues!" yelled the owner of the
tambourine
She taught the girl how to play it instead.